# THE POPSICLE COOKBOOK

## ICE POP AND POPSICLE RECIPES FOR 50 DELICIOUS FROZEN DESSERTS

By
BookSumo Press

Published by
BookSumo Press, a DBA of Saxonberg Associates
http://www.booksumo.com/

# ABOUT THE AUTHOR.

BookSumo Press is a publisher of unique, easy, and healthy cookbooks.

Our cookbooks span all topics and all subjects. If you want a deep dive into the possibilities of cooking with any type of ingredient. Then BookSumo Press is your go to place for robust yet simple and delicious cookbooks and recipes. Whether you are looking for great tasting pressure cooker recipes or authentic ethic and cultural food. BookSumo Press has a delicious and easy cookbook for you.

With simple ingredients, and even simpler step-by-step instructions BookSumo cookbooks get everyone in the kitchen chefing delicious meals.

BookSumo is an independent publisher of books operating in the beautiful Garden State (NJ) and our team of chefs and kitchen experts are here to teach, eat, and be merry!

# INTRODUCTION

Welcome to *The Effortless Chef Series*! Thank you for taking the time to purchase this cookbook.

Come take a journey into the delights of easy cooking. The point of this cookbook and all BookSumo Press cookbooks is to exemplify the effortless nature of cooking simply.

In this book we focus on Popsicle. You will find that even though the recipes are simple, the taste of the dishes are quite amazing.

So will you take an adventure in simple cooking? If the answer is yes please consult the table of contents to find the dishes you are most interested in.

Once you are ready, jump right in and start cooking.

— BookSumo Press

# TABLE OF CONTENTS

# Any Issues? Contact Us

If you find that something important to you is missing from this book please contact us at info@booksumo.com.

We will take your concerns into consideration when the 2nd edition of this book is published. And we will keep you updated!

— BookSumo Press

# Legal Notes

# COMMON ABBREVIATIONS

| cup(s) | C. |
|--------|-----|
| tablespoon | tbsp |
| teaspoon | tsp |
| ounce | oz. |
| pound | lb |

*All units used are standard American measurements

# Chapter 1: Easy Popsicle Recipes

# The Caribbean Pop

# (Vanilla and Pineapple)

## Ingredients

- 1 quart buttermilk
- 1 (20 oz.) can mixed fruit, drained
- 1 1/2 C. sugar
- 1 tsp vanilla extract
- 1/2 tsp salt
- 18 -20 paper C.
- 18 -20 wooden popsicle sticks or 18 -20 popsicle molds

## Directions

- Get a bowl, combine: salt, buttermilk, vanilla, sugar, and mixed fruit. Stir the mix until the salt is dissolved completely then divide the mix between ice pop molds.
- Partially freeze your ice pops then place a stick into each one and fully freeze them.
- Enjoy.

Amount per serving: 6

Timing Information:

| Preparation | 10 mins |
|---|---|
| Total Time | 10 mins |

Nutritional Information:

| Calories | 376.9 |
|---|---|
| Fat | 17.4g |
| Cholesterol | 0.0mg |
| Sodium | 7.4mg |
| Carbohydrates | 62.7g |
| Protein | 3.6g |

* Percent Daily Values are based on a 2,000 calorie diet.

# THE BRITISH POP
# (EARL GREY TEA AND SWEET MILK)

Ingredients

- 1 (12 oz.) cans evaporated milk
- 4 Earl Grey teabags
- 1/2 tsp ground cardamom
- 1 (14 oz.) cans sweetened condensed milk
- 1 C. heavy cream
- finely chopped pistachios

Directions

- Begin to heat your milk in a small pot until bubbles begin to show around the edges.
- At the same time remove the top part of your tea bags and combine the tea with the milk.
- Add in the cardamom with the milk.
- At this point the milk should be gently boiling, shut of the heat, place a lid on the pot and let the milk sit for 35 mins.

- Now run the milk through a strainer into a bowl then add in the condensed milk, pistachios, and cream.
- Divide this mix between the popsicle molds and cover the molds with some plastic wrap.
- Place everything in the freezer and let the mix sit in the freezer for 8 hours.
- Place the mold under some warm water before serving the popsicles.
- Top your popsicles with some nuts.
- Enjoy.

Amount per serving: 6

Timing Information:

| Preparation | 12 hrs 6 mins |
|---|---|
| Total Time | 17 hrs 6 mins |

Nutritional Information:

| Calories | 425.7 |
|---|---|
| Fat | 24.7g |
| Cholesterol | 93.2mg |
| Sodium | 159.2mg |
| Carbohydrates | 42.9g |
| Protein | 9.9g |

* Percent Daily Values are based on a 2,000 calorie diet.

# The Countryside Pop
# (Blueberries and Cream)

Ingredients

- 2/3 C. sugar, divided
- 3 tbsps fresh lemon juice, divided
- 3 C. fresh blueberries
- 1 C. peeled pitted, and sliced peach
- 1/3 C. heavy whipping cream

Directions

- Add the following to a food processor and pulse everything until it is evenly combined: berries, 2 tbsps lemon juice, and 3 tbsps sugar.
- Run the mix through a strainer into a big bowl and throw away any solid parts.
- Now add the rest of the juice (1 tbsp) and the peach to the food processor and pulse the mix again until it is evenly combined.
- Get a 2nd big bowl and add your cream to it then begin to process the cream with an electric mixer at the highest speed setting until

it begins to peak then add in your sugar and continue beating the mix until it is peaking again.

- Combine 1/4 of the whipped cream into the peach mix then add in the rest of the cream mix and place everything in the fridge to get cold.
- Now take your blueberry mix and divide it between 10 ice pop molds.
- Place the pops in the freezer for 30 mins.
- Remove the covers on the pop molds and coat the ice pops with the peach mix then place the lid on the molds again.
- Place in your sticks then place everything in the freezer again for 40 mins.
- Now remove the lids from the ice pops and cover them with the blueberry mix.
- Place the lids back on the ice pops and put them in the freezer for at least 5 hrs to get completely frozen.
- Enjoy

Amount per serving: 10

Timing Information:

| Preparation | 20 mins |
|---|---|
| Total Time | 20 mins |

Nutritional Information:

| Calories | 111.2 |
|---|---|
| Fat | 3.1g |
| Cholesterol | 10.8mg |
| Sodium | 3.6mg |
| Carbohydrates | 21.7g |
| Protein | 0.6g |

* Percent Daily Values are based on a 2,000 calorie diet.

# THE TOPICAL POP

# (BANANAS AND CHOCOLATE)

Ingredients

- 3 bananas
- 6 oz. half a bag chocolate chips
- 1 pinch nutmeg
- 1 dash cinnamon
- 1 tbsp milk
- 1 tbsp icing sugar

Directions

- Remove the skins of your bananas then place them to the side.
- Add your chips into a small pot and heat the chips until they are melted evenly.
- Combine in the cinnamon and nutmeg and shut the heat.
- Get a plate and line it with some parchment paper then layer your bananas on top of the parchment paper.

- Top the bananas with the chocolate and try to cover the fruits nicely.
- Now freeze everything for 40 mins.
- Top your frozen bananas with some icing sugar and insert a stick into each one.
- Enjoy.

Amount per serving: 3

Timing Information:

| Preparation | 10 mins |
|---|---|
| Total Time | 40 mins |

Nutritional Information:

| Calories | 376.9 |
|---|---|
| Fat | 17.4g |
| Cholesterol | 0.0mg |
| Sodium | 7.4mg |
| Carbohydrates | 62.7g |
| Protein | 3.6g |

* Percent Daily Values are based on a 2,000 calorie diet.

# THE LATIN POP

# (AVOCADOES AND LIME)

Ingredients

- 1 C. water
- 1/2 C. sugar
- 2 small ripe avocados

- 1 pinch salt
- 2 tbsps freshly squeezed lime juice

Directions

- Add your sugar and water to a small pot then begin to heat and stir the mix until everything is boiling.
- Once the sugar is completely combined shut the heat and let the mix get to room temp.
- Now slice your avocados into two pieces then take out the pit and remove the flesh into a food processor.
- Add in the room temp. syrup and some salt.
- Pulse the mix until it is combined nicely then add in the lime juice.
- Separate your avocado mix between ice pop molds then seal them with the lids and place everything in the freezer for 6 hrs. Enjoy.

Amount per serving: 8

Timing Information:

| Preparation | 15 mins |
|---|---|
| Total Time | 15 mins |

Nutritional Information:

| Calories | 121.6 |
|---|---|
| Fat | 6.6g |
| Cholesterol | 0.0mg |
| Sodium | 23.6mg |
| Carbohydrates | 16.6g |
| Protein | 0.9g |

* Percent Daily Values are based on a 2,000 calorie diet.

# The Orange and Green Machine Pop (Oranges, Kiwis, and Strawberry)

Ingredients

- 1 C. strawberry, hulled
- 2 large kiwi fruits, peeled
- 1/2 C. raspberries
- 1 1/2 C. orange juice

Directions

- Cut your kiwi and strawberries into 12 pieces and divide the pieces between 6 C.
- Slice the remaining fruit and divide them between the C. as well evenly.
- Now divide your orange juice between the C. and fill them and put everything in the freezer.
- After 65 mins of freezer time stake a stick into each C. And continue to freeze everything for 4 more hours.
- At serving time run the C. under some warm water and remove the popsicle.
- Enjoy.

Amount per serving: 6

Timing Information:

| Preparation | 20 mins |
|---|---|
| Total Time | 20 mins |

Nutritional Information:

| Calories | 59.4 |
|---|---|
| Fat | 0.4g |
| Cholesterol | 0.0mg |
| Sodium | 1.8mg |
| Carbohydrates | 13.9g |
| Protein | 1.0g |

* Percent Daily Values are based on a 2,000 calorie diet.

# THE SWEETY PIE POP
# (ORANGES, CHERRIES, AND YOGURT)

Ingredients

- 32 oz. yogurt
- 2 bananas
- 1/4 C. chopped maraschino cherry
- 1/2 C. approximately crushed pineapple in juice, undrained
- 1 tbsp approximately lemon juice
- 15 oz. mandarin oranges, drained, chopped
- 1/2 C. sugar

Directions

- Add your bananas to a food processor and pulse them until they are pureed nicely.
- Add the bananas to a bowl and add in the rest of the ingredients.
- Stir the mix to combine everything nicely then carefully divide the mix between ice pop molds.
- Place your pops in the freezer for 60 mins.
- Now stake your sticks into the molds and continue to freeze them until they are solid. Enjoy.

Amount per serving: 1

Timing Information:

| Preparation | 4 hrs |
|---|---|
| Total Time | 4 hrs |

Nutritional Information:

| Calories | 91.1 |
|---|---|
| Fat | 2.0g |
| Cholesterol | 7.4mg |
| Sodium | 27.1mg |
| Carbohydrates | 17.1g |
| Protein | 2.3g |

* Percent Daily Values are based on a 2,000 calorie diet.

# THE PINK POP
# (SWEET WATERMELON)

Ingredients

- 1 tbsp gelatin
- 1/4 C. boiling water
- 1/2 seedless watermelon
- 1/2 C. granulated sugar
- 1 tbsp fresh lemon juice or 1 tbsp lime juice

Directions

- Add your boiling water to a bowl and add your gelatin on top of the water.
- Let the mix sit for 65 secs.
- With a scooper take out the flesh of your watermelon and divide the insides of the fruit between 4 C.
- Add your melon, lemon juice, and sugar to a blender and pulse the mix a few times.

- Combine the melon mix with your gelatin mix and stir everything again then divide the mix between ice pop molds and place the sticks into the molds immediately.
- Place everything in the freezer for at least 4 hours.
- Enjoy.

Amount per serving: 1

Timing Information:

| Preparation | 15 mins |
|---|---|
| Total Time | 17 mins |

Nutritional Information:

| Calories | 68.2 |
|---|---|
| Fat | 0.2g |
| Cholesterol | 0.0mg |
| Sodium | 2.4mg |
| Carbohydrates | 16.9g |
| Protein | 1.2g |

* Percent Daily Values are based on a 2,000 calorie diet.

# THE BROWN AND PINK POP
# (CHOCOLATE WATERMELON)

Ingredients

- 1 small watermelon, seedless
- 1 C. sugar
- 1/2 C. mini chocolate chip
- 2 pt. lime sherbet, softened

Directions

- Remove the flesh of your watermelon and divide it between 10 C.
- Add the melon to a blender and also add in the sugar, working in batches, pulse the mix into an even puree.
- Now run the mix through a strainer into a bowl then place a covering on the bowl and put everything in the freezer for about 3 hours until it is partly frozen.
- Add in the chocolate pieces.
- Divide the mix between 24 plastic C. evenly, leaving about 1 inch of space, then put everything back in the freezer for 3 more hours.

- Divide your sherbet over each C. evenly, and place a covering of plastic over each one.
- Cut an opening into the covering and stake a stick into each C. carefully.
- Push the stick in as far as possible to increase its strength.
- Place everything back in the freezer overnight for up to 48 hours.
- Enjoy.

Amount per serving: 24

Timing Information:

| Preparation | 30 mins |
|---|---|
| Total Time | 11 hrs 30 mins |

Nutritional Information:

| Calories | 135.9 |
|---|---|
| Fat | 1.8g |
| Cholesterol | 0.2mg |
| Sodium | 13.5mg |
| Carbohydrates | 30.9g |
| Protein | 1.4g |

* Percent Daily Values are based on a 2,000 calorie diet.

# THE UNITED STATES OF POP
# (SUGAR CONES AND YOGURT)

Ingredients

- 3 C. vanilla yogurt
- red food coloring
- white food coloring
- blue food coloring
- wax paper
- 6 sugar ice cream cones
- 6 wooden popsicle sticks

Directions

- Add some red food coloring to half a 1/2 C. of yogurt and color 1.5 C. of yogurt with blue food coloring.
- Keep the remaining yogurt white.
- Lay out 6 pieces of wax paper that are about 1 foot in size.
- Fold them into triangles.
- Use each triangle as a covering for your sugar cones and tape them to the cone to preserve the structure.
- Add 1 tbsps of red yogurt, 2 tbsps of white, and 3 tbsps of blue.
- Add in your stick and place everything in the freezer for 5 hrs.
- Enjoy.

Amount per serving: 6

Timing Information:

| Preparation | 5 mins |
|---|---|
| Total Time | 4 hrs 5 mins |

Nutritional Information:

| Calories | 114.9 |
|---|---|
| Fat | 4.3g |
| Cholesterol | 15.9mg |
| Sodium | 88.3mg |
| Carbohydrates | 14.1g |
| Protein | 5.0g |

* Percent Daily Values are based on a 2,000 calorie diet.

# THE SOPHIA POP

# (HONEY AND FRUIT)

Ingredients

- 1 C. plain yogurt
- 1 C. fresh fruit
- 2 tbsps honey
- 4 wooden popsicle sticks
- 4 paper C., 5 oz. size
- aluminum foil

Directions

- Add the following to a food processor: honey, fruit, and yogurt. Pulse the mix until it is smooth then divide the mix between C. leaving about 1/4 of space in each C.
- Place a covering on each cut and slice a little opening into each one.
- Stake your sticks into each C. carefully then put everything in the fridge for 6 hours.
- Enjoy.

Amount per serving: 4

Timing Information:

| Preparation | 5 mins |
|---|---|
| Total Time | 5 hrs 5 mins |

Nutritional Information:

| Calories | 69.2 |
|---|---|
| Fat | 1.9g |
| Cholesterol | 7.9mg |
| Sodium | 28.6mg |
| Carbohydrates | 11.5g |
| Protein | 2.1g |

* Percent Daily Values are based on a 2,000 calorie diet.

# THE CHEESECAKE POP
# (CREAM CHEESE AND COOKIES)

Ingredients

- 4 oz. cream cheese
- 1/2 C. confectioners' sugar
- 1 C. heavy whipping cream
- 10 Oreo cookies

Directions

- Add the following to a stand mixer: confectioners' sugar and cream cheese.
- Whisk the mix with a medium level of intensity until everything is evenly combined.
- Set the speed to low then add in your cream and work the mix for a few mins then place the bowl into the freezer for an hour.
- Stir the mix everything 20 mins to keep it slightly soft.
- Dice or crush 5 Oreos then add the remaining Oreos to a blender and powder them with enough pulses.

- Add your cookies to the cream cheese mix and stir everything then divide the mix between ice pop molds.
- Place the molds back in the freezer for 5 hrs.
- Coat the ice pops with more crumbs.
- Enjoy.

Amount per serving: 8

Timing Information:

| Preparation | 15 mins |
|---|---|
| Total Time | 3 hrs 15 mins |

Nutritional Information:

| Calories | 247.8 |
|---|---|
| Fat | 18.7g |
| Cholesterol | 56.3mg |
| Sodium | 129.3mg |
| Carbohydrates | 19.0g |
| Protein | 2.2g |

* Percent Daily Values are based on a 2,000 calorie diet.

# THE BROWN TOWN POP

# (BUTTERY FUDGE AND VANILLA)

Ingredients

- 1/2 C. sugar
- 2 tbsps cornstarch
- 2 tbsps cocoa powder
- 2 1/2 C. milk
- 1 tsp vanilla
- 1 tbsp butter

Directions

- Add the following to a small pot: milk, sugar, cocoa, and cornstarch.
- Heat the mix until it is thick. Then shut the heat and combine in the butter and vanilla.
- Stir the mix until it is smooth then divide everything between ice pop molds.
- Place everything in the freezer until it is completely solid.
- Enjoy.

Amount per serving: 1

Timing Information:

| Preparation | 10 mins |
|---|---|
| Total Time | 10 mins |

Nutritional Information:

| Calories | 165.3 |
|---|---|
| Fat | 5.8g |
| Cholesterol | 19.3mg |
| Sodium | 67.1mg |
| Carbohydrates | 24.9g |
| Protein | 3.7g |

* Percent Daily Values are based on a 2,000 calorie diet.

# THE CLASSICAL POP
# (SWEET STRAWBERRIES)

Ingredients

- 1 C. mashed strawberry
- 1/2 C. water
- 3 tbsps sugar
- juice of half lime

Directions

- Get a bowl and combine all the ingredients: strawberry, water, sugar, and lime.
- Stir the mix until it is smooth then divide everything between ice pop molds.
- Place the molds in the freezer then freeze them until they are completely solid.
- Enjoy.

Amount per serving: 4

Timing Information:

| Preparation | 5 mins |
|---|---|
| Total Time | 5 mins |

Nutritional Information:

| Calories | 48.0 |
|---|---|
| Fat | 0.1g |
| Cholesterol | 0.0mg |
| Sodium | 1.3mg |
| Carbohydrates | 12.2g |
| Protein | 0.2g |

* Percent Daily Values are based on a 2,000 calorie diet.

# EASY PEASEY BERRY POP

Ingredients

- 3/4 C. fresh strawberries, hulled
- 1/4 C. sugar
- 1/2 C. water

Directions

- Add the following to the bowl of a food processor: strawberries, sugar, and water.
- Puree the mix evenly them then divide everything between 8 ice pop molds.
- Place everything in the freezer for about 4 hours.
- Enjoy.

Amount per serving: 8

Timing Information:

| Preparation | 5 mins |
|---|---|
| Total Time | 3 hrs 5 mins |

Nutritional Information:

| Calories | 28.5 |
|---|---|
| Fat | 0.0g |
| Cholesterol | 0.0mg |
| Sodium | 0.6mg |
| Carbohydrates | 7.2g |
| Protein | 0.0g |

* Percent Daily Values are based on a 2,000 calorie diet.

# THE RASTA POP
# (COCONUT AND PINEAPPLE)

Ingredients

- 1 1/4 C. pineapple juice
- 1 C. coconut milk
- 1 1/2 tbsps Splenda sugar substitute

Directions

- Add the following to a bowl, and stir everything until it is smooth: milk, pineapple juice, and sugar substitute.
- Stir the mix again then divide everything between ice pop molds.
- Place everything in the freezer for 8 hrs.
- Enjoy.

Amount per serving: 8

Timing Information:

| Preparation | 5 mins |
|---|---|
| Total Time | 4 hrs 5 mins |

Nutritional Information:

| Calories | 155.0 |
|---|---|
| Fat | 6.0g |
| Cholesterol | 0.0mg |
| Sodium | 14.1mg |
| Carbohydrates | 25.3g |
| Protein | 0.5g |

\* Percent Daily Values are based on a 2,000 calorie diet.

# THE BLUUUU POP
# (SYRUP AND BLUEBERRY)

Ingredients

- 1 pt. fresh blueberries
- 1 C. vanilla yogurt
- 1 C. milk
- sugar or honey or maple syrup, to taste

Directions

- Add the following to a bowl of a food processor: sugar, blueberries, milk, and yogurt.
- Pulse the mix until it is nicely pureed then divide the mix between 8 plastic C.
- Place a covering of plastic over each C. and cut slit a slit into each.
- Insert a stick into each C. and push it all the way to the bottom.
- Place everything in the freezer for 7 hrs.
- Enjoy.

Amount per serving: 8

Timing Information:

| Preparation | 10 mins |
|---|---|
| Total Time | 6 hrs 10 mins |

Nutritional Information:

| Calories | 58.7 |
|---|---|
| Fat | 2.2g |
| Cholesterol | 8.2mg |
| Sodium | 29.3mg |
| Carbohydrates | 8.0g |
| Protein | 2.3g |

* Percent Daily Values are based on a 2,000 calorie diet.

# THE SUMMER SOLSTICE POP

Ingredients

- 1 1/2 C. diced watermelon
- 1 C. orange juice
- 1 C. water
- 1/4 C. sugar

Directions

- Add your orange juice to blender and combine in the sugar.
- Stir the mix until the sugar is completely combined then place everything into the bowl of a blender with the watermelon and water as well.
- Pulse the mix until it is smooth and divide the mix between ice pop moulds.
- Place everything in the freezer overnight.
- Enjoy.

Amount per serving: 1

Timing Information:

| Preparation | 5 mins |
|---|---|
| Total Time | 5 mins |

Nutritional Information:

| Calories | 31.1 |
|---|---|
| Fat | 0.0g |
| Cholesterol | 0.0mg |
| Sodium | 0.7mg |
| Carbohydrates | 7.7g |
| Protein | 0.2g |

* Percent Daily Values are based on a 2,000 calorie diet.

# THE NUTTY FRUITY POP

Ingredients

- 5 bananas, just ripe
- 10 wooden popsicle sticks
- 1 C. peanuts, finely chopped
- 3 C. chocolate syrup, dark hard shell

Directions

- Cut your bananas into two pieces each then place a stick into each one.
- Coat each banana with the chocolate then roll each one in the nuts.
- Place everything in the freezer for 4 hours.
- Enjoy.

Amount per serving: 10

Timing Information:

| Preparation | 15 mins |
|---|---|
| Total Time | 3 hrs 15 mins |

Nutritional Information:

| Calories | 454.4 |
|---|---|
| Fat | 15.5g |
| Cholesterol | 0.9mg |
| Sodium | 318.7mg |
| Carbohydrates | 73.2g |
| Protein | 8.6g |

* Percent Daily Values are based on a 2,000 calorie diet.

# THE MANDARIN POP

Ingredients

- 16 oz. vanilla yogurt
- 2 tsps vanilla
- 1 (6 oz.) cans frozen orange juice concentrate

Directions

- Add the following ingredients to a bowl, and stir everything until it is smooth: yogurt, vanilla, and concentrate.
- Once the mix is smooth evenly divide everything between plastic C.
- Cover each C. with plastic wrap and cut a slit into each one.
- Insert a stick into each one and place everything in the freezer overnight.
- Enjoy.

Amount per serving: 6

Timing Information:

| Preparation | 10 mins |
|---|---|
| Total Time | 10 mins |

Nutritional Information:

| Calories | 106.9 |
|---|---|
| Fat | 2.5g |
| Cholesterol | 9.9mg |
| Sodium | 36.2mg |
| Carbohydrates | 17.2g |
| Protein | 3.4g |

* Percent Daily Values are based on a 2,000 calorie diet.

# THE BAHAMIAN POP

Ingredients

- 1 1/4 C. mangoes, chopped
- 3/4 C. coconut milk
- 1 tbsp sugar
- 1 tbsp lime juice

Directions

- Add the following to the bowl of a food processor: lime juice, mango, sugar, and coconut milk.
- Pulse the mix until it is smooth then add in some more sugar if you like.
- Divide the mix between ice pop moulds and freeze them overnight or at least 5 hours.
- Enjoy.

Amount per serving: 6

Timing Information:

| Preparation | 20 mins |
|---|---|
| Total Time | 6 hrs 20 mins |

Nutritional Information:

| Calories | 161.4 |
|---|---|
| Fat | 6.1g |
| Cholesterol | 0.0mg |
| Sodium | 13.7mg |
| Carbohydrates | 27.1g |
| Protein | 0.7g |

* Percent Daily Values are based on a 2,000 calorie diet.

# THE RAZZ-MA-TAZZ POP
# (ICE CREAM, CHOCOLATE, AND STRAWBERRY)

Ingredients

- 1 pt. strawberry
- 1 pt. fat free cream
- low-fat chocolate

Directions

- Add your ice cream to a bowl then add in the whipped cream and strawberries.
- Stir everything evenly. Then divide the mix between small Dixie C.
- Place a stick into each C. and insert it all the way to the bottom.
- Place everything in the freezer overnight.
- Top the popsicles with some chocolate sauce.
- Enjoy.

Amount per serving: 14

Timing Information:

| Preparation | 7 mins |
|---|---|
| Total Time | 7 mins |

Nutritional Information:

| Calories | 28.5 |
|---|---|
| Fat | 0.5g |
| Cholesterol | 1.7mg |
| Sodium | 50.0mg |
| Carbohydrates | 5.0g |
| Protein | 1.0g |

\* Percent Daily Values are based on a 2,000 calorie diet.

# A Pop from the Tropics

Ingredients

- 1 C. pineapple juice
- 1 banana
- 1/4 C. coconut, shredded
- 4 paper C., dixie
- 4 wooden popsicle sticks

Directions

- Add the following to the bowl of a food processor: banana and juice. With a high intensity pulse the mix until it is combined evenly then divide the mix between plastic C.
- Place a covering of plastic on each C. and slice a little hole into each one.
- Insert a stick into each C. all the way to the bottom.
- Place everything in the fridge for at least 6 hrs or preferably overnight.
- Enjoy.

Amount per serving: 4

Timing Information:

| Preparation | 5 mins |
|---|---|
| Total Time | 1 hr 5 mins |

Nutritional Information:

| Calories | 59.3 |
|---|---|
| Fat | 0.1g |
| Cholesterol | 0.0mg |
| Sodium | 1.5mg |
| Carbohydrates | 14.7g |
| Protein | 0.5g |

* Percent Daily Values are based on a 2,000 calorie diet.

# YELLOW AND GREEN POP

Ingredients

- 440 g crushed pineapple in natural juice
- 1/2 C. natural yoghurt
- 1 lime, juice of
- 2 tbsps brown sugar
- 8 wooden icy pole sticks

Directions

- Get a large pitcher and add in your pineapple juice, yogurt, lime, and brown sugar.
- Stir the mix evenly then divide everything between ice pop moulds.
- Place everything in the fridge for 8 hrs.
- Enjoy.

Amount per serving: 8

Timing Information:

| Preparation | 10 mins |
|-------------|---------|
| Total Time | 10 mins |

Nutritional Information:

| Calories | 24.9 |
|----------|------|
| Fat | 0.5g |
| Cholesterol | 1.9mg |
| Sodium | 8.1mg |
| Carbohydrates | 4.9g |
| Protein | 0.5g |

* Percent Daily Values are based on a 2,000 calorie diet.

# THE SPICY MEXICAN POP

# (CUCUMBERS, JALAPENOS, AND SUGAR)

Ingredients

- 3 C. cucumbers
- 2/3 C. sugar
- 1/3 C. lemon juice
- 1 jalapeno chile, seeds removed

Directions

- Add the following to the bowl of a food processor: cucumbers, sugar, lemon, and jalapeno.
- Pulse the mix until you have a puree then run everything through a strainer.
- Divide the mix between ice pop moulds and place everything in freezer overnight.
- Enjoy.

Amount per serving: 6

Timing Information:

| Preparation | 5 mins |
|---|---|
| Total Time | 8 hrs 5 mins |

Nutritional Information:

| Calories | 97.5 |
|---|---|
| Fat | 0.1g |
| Cholesterol | 0.0mg |
| Sodium | 1.4mg |
| Carbohydrates | 25.2g |
| Protein | 0.4g |

* Percent Daily Values are based on a 2,000 calorie diet.

# THE SWEETEST POP

Ingredients

- 1 (12 oz.) cans fruit nectar
- 4 paper C., dixie
- 4 wooden popsicle sticks

Directions

- Divide your nectar between small C. then place a covering of plastic on each C.
- Cut a small opening into each one then place a stick into each.
- Put everything in the freezer overnight.
- Enjoy.

Amount per serving: 4

Timing Information:

| Preparation | 2 mins |
|---|---|
| Total Time | 1 hr 2 mins |

Nutritional Information:

| Calories | 0.0 |
|---|---|
| Fat | 0.0g |
| Cholesterol | 0.0mg |
| Sodium | 0.0mg |
| Carbohydrates | 0.0g |
| Protein | 0.0g |

* Percent Daily Values are based on a 2,000 calorie diet.

# Easy Ice Pops

Ingredients

- ice cube
- 1 C. apple juice
- 2/3 C. club soda
- fresh fruit, for garnish

Directions

- Combine the fruit juice and club soda in a pitcher evenly then pour everything into plastic C. filling them halfway.
- Place a covering of plastic on each one.
- Insert a stick into each one and put everything in the freezer overnight.
- Enjoy.

Amount per serving: 1

Timing Information:

| Preparation | 5 mins |
|---|---|
| Total Time | 5 mins |

Nutritional Information:

| Calories | 0.0 |
|---|---|
| Fat | 0.0g |
| Cholesterol | 0.0mg |
| Sodium | 16.5mg |
| Carbohydrates | 0.0g |
| Protein | 0.0g |

* Percent Daily Values are based on a 2,000 calorie diet.

# A Real Rustic Pop

# (Rosemary and Apples)

Ingredients

- 4 C. apple juice
- 1/2 C. water
- 1/2 C. sugar
- 2 tbsps chopped fresh rosemary
- 1 cinnamon stick, broken in half
- 2 whole cloves
- 4 tsps apple cider vinegar
- 1/4 tsp vanilla extract

Directions

- Get the following boiling in a large pot: apple juice, water, sugar, rosemary, cinnamon stick, and cloves.
- Let the mix boil for 30 mins.
- Run everything through a strainer into a bowl then add in the vanilla and vinegar.
- Stir the mix evenly then place everything into ice pop moulds.
- Place the molds in the freezer for 8 hrs.
- Enjoy.

Amount per serving: 1

Timing Information:

| Preparation | 45 mins |
|---|---|
| Total Time | 45 mins |

Nutritional Information:

| Calories | 72.3 |
|---|---|
| Fat | 0.1g |
| Cholesterol | 0.0mg |
| Sodium | 4.7mg |
| Carbohydrates | 17.9g |
| Protein | 0.1g |

* Percent Daily Values are based on a 2,000 calorie diet.

# SUNSHINE POP

Ingredients

- 1/2 C. cranberry juice cocktail
- 2 tbsps lime juice
- 2 tsps honey
- 1 1/2 C. orange juice
- 1/4 C. tequila

Directions

- Add the following to a measuring C.: honey, lime juice, and cranberry juice.
- Add about 4 tsps of mixture into eight ice pop moulds.
- Place the moulds in the freezer for 65 mins.
- Now add your tequila and orange juice to another small bowl then enter the mix on top of the cranberry mix.
- Place everything back in the freezer for 8 hours.
- Enjoy.

Amount per serving: 1

Timing Information:

| Preparation | 15 mins |
|---|---|
| Total Time | 15 mins |

Nutritional Information:

| Calories | 35.6 |
|---|---|
| Fat | 0.1g |
| Cholesterol | 0.0mg |
| Sodium | 0.9mg |
| Carbohydrates | 8.7g |
| Protein | 0.3g |

* Percent Daily Values are based on a 2,000 calorie diet.

# THE LITTLE RED POP

Ingredients

- 2 mangoes
- 5 tbsps icing sugar
- 40 ml cranberry juice

Directions

- Hull your mangoes and cut each one into 4 pieces.
- Add the fruit to the bowl of your food processor pulse it into a puree then combine in the cranberry juice and the icing sugar.
- Continue to process the mix for 1 more mins then run everything through a sieve or fine strainer.
- Throw away the resulting solids then divide everything between ice pop moulds evenly.
- Place everything in the freezer for a whole day and night.
- Enjoy.

Amount per serving: 4

Timing Information:

| Preparation | 7 mins |
|---|---|
| Total Time | 24 hrs 7 mins |

Nutritional Information:

| Calories | 223.1 |
|---|---|
| Fat | 0.6g |
| Cholesterol | 0.0mg |
| Sodium | 2.4mg |
| Carbohydrates | 56.5g |
| Protein | 1.3g |

* Percent Daily Values are based on a 2,000 calorie diet.

# SIMPLE CRANBERRY POPS

Ingredients

- 1 pineapple
- 5 tbsps icing sugar
- 40 ml cranberry juice

Directions

- Remove the skins of your pineapple and slice into chunks.
- Add the fruit to the bowl of your food processor then pulse it into a puree then combine in the cranberry juice and the icing sugar.
- Continue to process the mix for 1 more mins then run everything through a sieve or fine strainer.
- Throw away the resulting solids then divide everything between ice pop moulds evenly.
- Place everything in the freezer for a whole day and night.
- Enjoy.

Amount per serving: 4

Timing Information:

| Preparation | 7 mins |
|---|---|
| Total Time | 24 hrs 7 mins |

Nutritional Information:

| Calories | 223.1 |
|---|---|
| Fat | 0.6g |
| Cholesterol | 0.0mg |
| Sodium | 2.4mg |
| Carbohydrates | 56.5g |
| Protein | 1.3g |

* Percent Daily Values are based on a 2,000 calorie diet.

# HONEY AND YOGURT POP

Ingredients

- 1/2 C. honey
- 1/4 C. fresh lemon juice
- two 6-oz. containers lemon low-calorie nonfat yogurt
- 1 1/2 C. blueberries

Directions

- Add the following to a small pot: lemon juice, and honey.
- Heat the mix while stirring for 5 mins then shut the heat and let the mix sit for 7 mins.
- Get a bowl and mix the honey mix with the yogurt and add in the blueberries.
- Divide the mix between ice pop moulds and put everything in the freezer for 5 hrs.
- Enjoy.

Amount per serving: 1

Timing Information:

| Preparation | 5 mins |
|---|---|
| Total Time | 10 mins |

Nutritional Information:

| Calories | 65.5 |
|---|---|
| Fat | 0.0g |
| Cholesterol | 0.0mg |
| Sodium | 0.9mg |
| Carbohydrates | 17.6g |
| Protein | 0.2g |

* Percent Daily Values are based on a 2,000 calorie diet.

# YELLOWSTONE STYLE POP

Ingredients

- 2 C. packed finely chopped seeded watermelon
- 0.5 (12 oz.) cans frozen lemonade concentrate, thawed (3/4 C.)
- 3 tbsps sugar
- 1 pinch salt

Directions

- Add the following to the bowl of a food processor: watermelon, lemon concentrate, sugar, and salt.
- Pulse the mix until it becomes a smooth puree then divide everything between eight ice pop molds evenly.
- Place everything in the freezer for 5 hrs.
- Enjoy.

Amount per serving: 1

Timing Information:

| Preparation | 10 mins |
|---|---|
| Total Time | 10 mins |

Nutritional Information:

| Calories | 79.2 |
|---|---|
| Fat | 0.1g |
| Cholesterol | 0.0mg |
| Sodium | 20.8mg |
| Carbohydrates | 20.4g |
| Protein | 0.3g |

* Percent Daily Values are based on a 2,000 calorie diet.

# PARISIAN POP

Ingredients

- 4 C. honeydew melon, peeled and ripe cut into 1/2-inch pieces
- 5 tbsps daiquiri
- 3 tbsps lemon lime soda
- 1 1/2 tbsps superfine sugar
- Special equipment
- 6 ice popsicle molds
- 6 wooden sticks

Directions

- Add the following to the bowl of a food processor and puree the mix until it is smooth: honeydew, daiquiri, lemon lime soda, and sugar.
- Run the mix through a sieve or fine strainer into a bowl and let it sit for 40 mins.
- Throw away the solids and divide the mix between ice pop moulds and place everything in the freezer for an entire day.
- Enjoy.

Amount per serving: 6

Timing Information:

| Preparation | 24 hrs |
| Total Time | 24 hrs |

Nutritional Information:

| Calories | 70.7 |
| Fat | 0.1g |
| Cholesterol | 0.0mg |
| Sodium | 21.3mg |
| Carbohydrates | 13.8g |
| Protein | 0.6g |

* Percent Daily Values are based on a 2,000 calorie diet.

# Milanese Strawberry Pop

Ingredients

- 1 C. strawberries
- 5 tbsps icing sugar
- 40 ml grape juice

Directions

- Hull your strawberries and cut them into 4 pieces each.
- Add the fruit to the bowl of your food processor then pulse it into a puree then combine in the grape juice and the icing sugar.
- Continue to process the mix for 1 more min then run everything through a sieve or fine strainer.
- Throw away the resulting solids then divide everything between ice pop moulds evenly.
- Place everything in the freezer for a whole day and night.
- Enjoy.

Amount per serving: 6

Timing Information:

| Preparation | 7 mins |
|---|---|
| Total Time | 24 hrs 7 mins |

Nutritional Information:

| Calories | 70.3 |
|---|---|
| Fat | 0.1g |
| Cholesterol | 0.0mg |
| Sodium | 1.3mg |
| Carbohydrates | 18.5g |
| Protein | 0.4g |

* Percent Daily Values are based on a 2,000 calorie diet.

# THE CIRCUS POPCORN POP

Ingredients

- 4 oz. scoop cookie dough ice cream
- 2 oz. caramel popped popcorn
- 1 flat wooden dessert stick

Directions

- Cot your scoop of ice cream with the popcorn then stake a stick through it.
- Place everything into the freezer for 4 hours after covering the pop with some plastic wrap.
- Enjoy.

Amount per serving: 1

Timing Information:

| Preparation | 5 mins |
|---|---|
| Total Time | 2 hrs 5 mins |

Nutritional Information:

| Calories | 0.0 |
|---|---|
| Fat | 0.0g |
| Cholesterol | 0.0mg |
| Sodium | 0.0mg |
| Carbohydrates | 0.0g |
| Protein | 0.0g |

* Percent Daily Values are based on a 2,000 calorie diet.

# THE POOLSIDE POP

## Ingredients

- 1 C. lime juice
- 1/2 C. water
- 1/2 C. lemon lime soda
- 1/4 C. fresh lemon juice
- 1/2 C. superfine sugar
- 1 pt. strawberry, quartered
- Special equipment
- 8 popsicle molds

## Directions

- Add the following to the bowl of a food processor: sugar, lemon juice, water, lime soda, and lime juice.
- Pulse the mix until it is smooth then add your strawberries saving two for later.
- Puree everything then add in the rest of the strawberries but pulse the mix to keep the strawberries a bit chunky.
- Divide the mix between ice pop molds and place everything in the freezer for 8 hrs.
- Enjoy.

Amount per serving: 8

Timing Information:

| Preparation | 10 mins |
| Total Time | 12 hrs 10 mins |

Nutritional Information:

| Calories | 70.3 |
| Fat | 0.1g |
| Cholesterol | 0.0mg |
| Sodium | 1.3mg |
| Carbohydrates | 18.5g |
| Protein | 0.4g |

* Percent Daily Values are based on a 2,000 calorie diet.

# THE TEA LEAVE POP

Ingredients

- 5 C. hot water
- 2 tbsps green tea
- 1/2 C. sugar

Directions

- Get your 4 C. of water boiling in a pot then add in the 5 tsp of tea leaves.
- Shut the heat and let the mix sit for 7 mins then run the tea through a strainer.
- Add in half a C. of sugar to the mix and run the tea through a strainer.
- Divide the mix between ice pop moulds then place everything in the freezer for at least 6 hrs or ideally overnight.
- Enjoy.

Amount per serving: 8

Timing Information:

| Preparation | 15 mins |
|---|---|
| Total Time | 5 hrs 15 mins |

Nutritional Information:

| Calories | 48.3 |
|---|---|
| Fat | 0.0g |
| Cholesterol | 0.0mg |
| Sodium | 2.9mg |
| Carbohydrates | 12.5g |
| Protein | 0.0g |

* Percent Daily Values are based on a 2,000 calorie diet.

# THE RASPY RASPBERRY POP

Ingredients

- 1 1/2 C. raspberries, fresh or frozen
- 1/2 C. sugar
- 1 egg white

Directions

- Add your raspberries, sugar, and egg whites, to the bowl of a food processor and puree them evenly.
- Divide the mix between Dixie C. then insert sticks into each one.
- Place everything in the freezer until completely frozen.
- Enjoy.

Amount per serving: 1

Timing Information:

| Preparation | 10 mins |
|---|---|
| Total Time | 10 mins |

Nutritional Information:

| Calories | 116.6 |
|---|---|
| Fat | 0.1g |
| Cholesterol | 0.0mg |
| Sodium | 0.6mg |
| Carbohydrates | 29.7g |
| Protein | 0.4g |

* Percent Daily Values are based on a 2,000 calorie diet.

# BLACKBERRY DREAM POP

Ingredients

- 1 1/2 C. blackberries
- 1/2 C. sugar
- 1 egg white

Directions

- Add your blackberries, sugar, and egg whites, to the bowl of a food processor and puree them evenly.
- Divide the mix between Dixie C. then add in your sticks to each one.
- Place everything in the freezer until completely frozen.
- Enjoy.

Amount per serving: 1

Timing Information:

| Preparation | 10 mins |
|---|---|
| Total Time | 10 mins |

Nutritional Information:

| Calories | 116.6 |
|---|---|
| Fat | 0.1g |
| Cholesterol | 0.0mg |
| Sodium | 0.6mg |
| Carbohydrates | 29.7g |
| Protein | 0.4g |

* Percent Daily Values are based on a 2,000 calorie diet.

# MICHELLE'S BUTTERMILK APPLE POP

Ingredients

- 1 quart buttermilk
- 1 (20 oz.) cans crushed pineapple, drained
- 1 1/2 C. sugar
- 1 tsp vanilla extract
- 1/2 tsp salt
- 18 -20 paper C.
- 18 -20 wooden popsicle sticks or 18 -20 popsicle molds

Directions

- Get a bowl, combine: salt, buttermilk, vanilla, sugar, and pineapple.
- Stir the mix until the salt is dissolved completely then divide the mix between ice pop moulds.
- Partially freeze your ice pops then place a stick into each one and fully freeze them.
- Enjoy.

Amount per serving: 18

Timing Information:

| Preparation | 10 mins |
| Total Time | 10 mins |

Nutritional Information:

| Calories | 105.8 |
| Fat | 0.5g |
| Cholesterol | 2.1mg |
| Sodium | 122.1mg |
| Carbohydrates | 24.2g |
| Protein | 1.9g |

* Percent Daily Values are based on a 2,000 calorie diet.

# THE CONCENTRATE POP

Ingredients

- 1 C. milk
- 1 pt. vanilla ice cream
- 1 (6 oz.) frozen concentrate orange juice

Directions

- Add the following to the bowl of a food processor: milk, ice cream, orange concentrate.
- Puree the mix until it is even and smooth then divide everything between plastic C.
- Put everything in the freezer for a few hours then add a stick to each one.
- Place everything back in the freezer until it is completely solid.
- Enjoy.

Amount per serving: 8

Timing Information:

| Preparation | 10 mins |
|---|---|
| Total Time | 10 mins |

Nutritional Information:

| Calories | 127.2 |
|---|---|
| Fat | 5.0g |
| Cholesterol | 19.9mg |
| Sodium | 44.2mg |
| Carbohydrates | 18.4g |
| Protein | 2.7g |

* Percent Daily Values are based on a 2,000 calorie diet.

# THE BIRCH BEER POP

Ingredients

- 4 C. root beer
- 6 maraschino cherries, stemmed
- 2 1/2 C. vanilla ice cream

Directions

- Add your root beer to a jug then place it in the freezer for 12 mins.
- Place a single cherry into each of your ice pop moulds then fill each one half way with cold root beer.
- Add a scoop of ice cream to one and leave about 25 percent of the moulds empty.
- Fill the remaining space with more soda then remove any froth from the soda with a spoon.
- Place everything in the freezer overnight.
- Enjoy

Amount per serving: 6

Timing Information:

| Preparation | 15 mins |
|---|---|
| Total Time | 15 mins |

Nutritional Information:

| Calories | 196.2 |
|---|---|
| Fat | 6.6g |
| Cholesterol | 26.4mg |
| Sodium | 69.5mg |
| Carbohydrates | 33.6g |
| Protein | 2.1g |

* Percent Daily Values are based on a 2,000 calorie diet.

# No Diary Pop

Ingredients

- 2 C. frozen mixed fruit
- 1 C. unsweetened coconut milk
- 3 tsps sugar

Directions

- Add the following to the bowl of a food processor and puree it: mixed fruit, coconut milk, and sugar.
- Puree the mix evenly then divide the mix evenly between little C. and place a stick into each one.
- Place everything in the freezer for 8 hours.
- Enjoy.

Amount per serving: 20

Timing Information:

| Preparation | 10 mins |
|---|---|
| Total Time | 24 hrs 10 mins |

Nutritional Information:

| Calories | 46.7 |
|---|---|
| Fat | 2.4g |
| Cholesterol | 0.0mg |
| Sodium | 2.2mg |
| Carbohydrates | 6.3g |
| Protein | 0.5g |

* Percent Daily Values are based on a 2,000 calorie diet.

# THE STATE FAIR POP

Ingredients

- 2 (270 ml) cans light coconut milk
- 250 g frozen mixed berries, roughly chopped
- 1/4 C. dark chocolate, coarsely grated
- 1/4 C. caster sugar

Directions

- Add the following to a bowl: coconut milk, berries, chocolate, and sugar.
- Stir the mix evenly then divide everything between ice pop moulds.
- Place everything in the freezer overnight.
- Enjoy.

Amount per serving: 6

Timing Information:

| Preparation | 2 mins |
|---|---|
| Total Time | 2 mins |

Nutritional Information:

| Calories | 59.8 |
|---|---|
| Fat | 2.8g |
| Cholesterol | 0.0mg |
| Sodium | 1.3mg |
| Carbohydrates | 9.9g |
| Protein | 0.7g |

* Percent Daily Values are based on a 2,000 calorie diet.

# Catalina's Cantaloupe Pop

Ingredients

- 1/2 ripe cantaloupe, peeled, seeds removed, cut into chunks
- 1/2 C. sugar
- 1 lime, zest of
- 1 1/2 tbsps fresh lime juice

Directions

- Add your cantaloupe to the bowl of a food processor and puree it.
- Puree the mix until you have about two C. of puree.
- Add the puree back into the bowl of the processor then combine in 3/4 C. of water, lime zest, sugar, and lime juice.
- Begin to pulse the mix again until it is combined evenly.
- Divide the mix between ice pop moulds and place everything in the freezer for 8 hrs.
- Enjoy.

Amount per serving: 8

Timing Information:

| Preparation | 20 mins |
|---|---|
| Total Time | 4 hrs 20 mins |

Nutritional Information:

| Calories | 60.7 |
|---|---|
| Fat | 0.0g |
| Cholesterol | 0.0mg |
| Sodium | 5.7mg |
| Carbohydrates | 15.5g |
| Protein | 0.3g |

* Percent Daily Values are based on a 2,000 calorie diet.

# Syrup and Cucumber Pop

Ingredients

- 1 large cucumber
- 1/2 C. fresh pineapple chunk
- 1/2 C. pineapple juice
- 1 tbsp simple syrup
- 1/2 C. fresh pineapple, diced and frozen

Directions

- Get a bowl and place a strainer over the bowl.
- Place a piece of cheesecloth in the strainer before doing anything else.
- Take your cucumber and grate it directly into the cheesecloth then press and squeeze the cloth to get the cucumber juice.
- Try to make about half a C. of juice. Then add the cucumber juice, pineapple chunks and juice, and syrup to the bowl of a food processor.
- Puree the mix evenly then divide everything between ice pop moulds.
- Place everything into the freezer overnight.
- Enjoy.

Amount per serving: 4

Timing Information:

| Preparation | 15 mins |
|---|---|
| Total Time | 15 mins |

Nutritional Information:

| Calories | 46.4 |
|---|---|
| Fat | 0.1g |
| Cholesterol | 0.0mg |
| Sodium | 2.5mg |
| Carbohydrates | 11.6g |
| Protein | 0.8g |

* Percent Daily Values are based on a 2,000 calorie diet.

# Mango Madness Pop

## (Nutmeg, Red Pepper, Oranges, and Mangoes)

Ingredients

- 2 large mangoes, flesh of
- 1 C. fresh orange juice
- 2 tbsps ginger juice
- 1/8 tsp ground red pepper
- 1 pinch cardamom
- 1/8 tsp grated nutmeg
- 1 pinch salt

Directions

- To make the ginger juice. Take a big piece of ginger and grate it completely. Squeeze the grated ginger to form the juice.
- Add the orange juice and mangoes to the bowl of a food processor and puree them. Then add the puree to a bowl with the salt, ginger juice, nutmeg, cardamom, and red pepper.
- Work the mix until the salt is evenly combined then divide everything between ice pop molds.
- Place everything in the freezer overnight. Enjoy.

Amount per serving: 6

Timing Information:

| Preparation | 15 mins |
|---|---|
| Total Time | 15 mins |

Nutritional Information:

| Calories | 73.0 |
|---|---|
| Fat | 0.3g |
| Cholesterol | 0.0mg |
| Sodium | 27.9mg |
| Carbohydrates | 18.4g |
| Protein | 0.7g |

\* Percent Daily Values are based on a 2,000 calorie diet.

# ELEGANT GRAPE POP

Ingredients

- 1 1/2 C. grapes, fresh
- 1/2 C. sugar
- 1 egg white

Directions

- Add your grapes, sugar, and egg whites, to the bowl of a food processor and puree them evenly.
- Divide the mix between Dixie C. then add in your sticks to each one. Place everything in the freezer until completely frozen.
- Enjoy.

Amount per serving: 1

Timing Information:

| Preparation | 10 mins |
|---|---|
| Total Time | 10 mins |

Nutritional Information:

| Calories | 116.6 |
|---|---|
| Fat | 0.1g |
| Cholesterol | 0.0mg |
| Sodium | 0.6mg |
| Carbohydrates | 29.7g |
| Protein | 0.4g |

* Percent Daily Values are based on a 2,000 calorie diet.

# WHITE AND YELLOW POP

Ingredients

- 1 quart buttermilk
- 1 (20 oz.) can peaches, drained
- 1 1/2 C. sugar
- 1 tsp vanilla extract
- 1/2 tsp salt
- 18 -20 paper C.
- 18 -20 wooden popsicle sticks or 18 -20 popsicle molds

Directions

- Get a bowl, combine: salt, buttermilk, vanilla, sugar, and peaches. Stir the mix until the salt is dissolved completely then divide the mix between ice pop moulds.
- Partially freeze your ice pops then place a stick into each one and fully freeze them.
- Enjoy.

Amount per serving: 6

Timing Information:

| Preparation | 10 mins |
|---|---|
| Total Time | 10 mins |

Nutritional Information:

| Calories | 116.6 |
|---|---|
| Fat | 0.1g |
| Cholesterol | 0.0mg |
| Sodium | 0.6mg |
| Carbohydrates | 29.7g |
| Protein | 0.4g |

* Percent Daily Values are based on a 2,000 calorie diet.

# Thanks for Reading! Join the Club and Keep on Cooking with 6 More Cookbooks....

http://bit.ly/1TdrStv

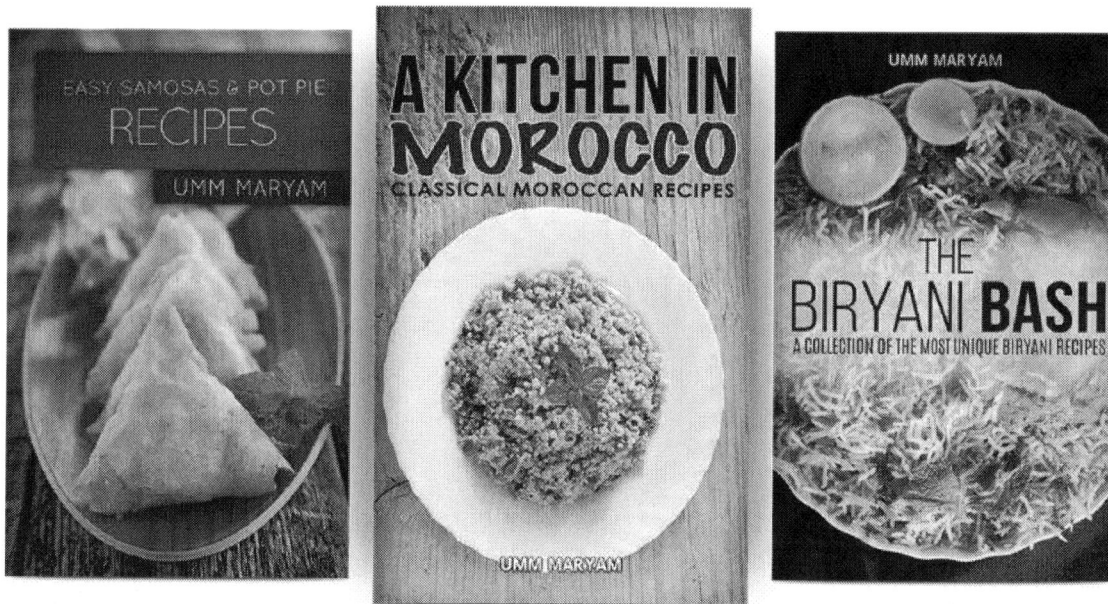

EASY SAMOSAS & POT PIE
RECIPES

UMM MARYAM

A KITCHEN IN
MOROCCO
CLASSICAL MOROCCAN RECIPES

UMM MARYAM

UMM MARYAM

THE
BIRYANI BASH
A COLLECTION OF THE MOST UNIQUE BIRYANI RECIPES

To grab the box sets simply follow the link mentioned above, or tap one of book covers.

This will take you to a page where you can simply enter your email address and a PDF version of the box sets will be emailed to you.

Hope you are ready for some serious cooking!

http://bit.ly/1TdrStv

# COME ON...
# LET'S BE FRIENDS : )

We adore our readers and love connecting with them socially.

Like BookSumo on Facebook and let's get social!

Facebook

And also check out the BookSumo Cooking Blog.

Food Lover Blog

Printed in Great Britain
by Amazon